SEVEN ANGELS

Seven practical tips to becoming a good leader

DAMRONG PINKOON

JAICO PUBLISHING HOUSE

Ahmedabad Bangalore Bhopal Bhubaneswar Chennai
Delhi Hyderabad Kolkata Lucknow Mumbai

Published by Jaico Publishing House
A-2 Jash Chambers, 7-A Sir Phirozshah Mehta Road
Fort, Mumbai - 400 001
jaicopub@jaicobooks.com
www.jaicobooks.com

Published in arrangement with
Damrong Pinkoon Company Limited
999 Gaysorn Plaza 5th Floor, Lumpini
Pathumwan, Bangkok 10330, Thailand

SEVEN ANGELS
ISBN 978-81-8495-673-3

First Jaico Impression: 2015

Printed by
Rashmi Graphics
#3, Amrutwel CHS Ltd., C.S. #50/74
Ganesh Galli, Lalbaug, Mumbai - 400 012
E-mail: rashmigraphics84@gmail.com

SEVEN ANGELS

Seven practical tips for becoming a good leader

Author's Preface

Many people
want to be good leaders.
Luckily for them, it's not a tall order to be one.

Many people
endlessly seek shortcuts
to learn how to become successful leaders.
To some, being a good leader comes naturally,
while for many others it is not so easy
because they were not born with the requisite skills.

Thankfully, the Seven Angels
can show aspiring leaders the right paths
to take so that they may become both
happy and successful leaders.

All human beings
are blessed with latent leadership energy,
but when the right time comes,
only a few can tap into
this suppressed power efficiently.

Publisher's Preface

Various excellent and positive stories
have been creatively depicted by veteran
and prolific author, Damrong Pinkoon.

The tale of the Seven Angels
is vibrantly portrayed through the story of
a great Roman commander-in-chief's son,
who aspired to be
a good leader like his father.

The leadership lessons this young man learns
are as useful and valuable today,
as they were then.
During his journey, he meets
a group of seven angels
who kindly teach him
how to become a good leader
of the Roman army.

A great leader's lessons

demonstrate his great work.

Any person

who has had enriching experiences

can become a successful leader.

1

A ROMAN COMMANDER-IN-CHIEF

During the glorious days of the Roman Empire, King Autopus was considered one of the most valiant and capable leaders. He had an indomitable and mighty army that had many lion-hearted commander-in-chiefs. They could lead a legion of soldiers to vanquish other kingdoms.

At the end of every war, King Autopus granted special rewards to any general who defeated his enemies.

Such a kind gesture from the king brought great pride to all triumphant generals. His benevolence also inspired soldiers to follow in the footsteps of their commanders, so that they would be admired by the citizens too.

Among the many brave generals of the Roman army, Soratus was regarded as one of the greatest. He conquered many armies, and so, was highly respected by the young army leaders. It was widely believed that Rome maintained her glory thanks to Soratus's capabilities and heroic deeds.

Now, the legendary Soratus had reached his retirement. He could no longer serve in the army. Yet, many commanders still approached him to seek his useful advice.

Soratus recalled countless legends about the wars he had fought because he had played a vital role in strengthening the Roman Empire.

Since Soratus could no longer lead the army, King Autopus was concerned about its future.

Given the seriousness of the impending situation, the king invited Soratus to his palace and asked him to select the next great commander-in-chief, who would lead the soldiers and also serve as the army's pillar.

When Soratus arrived at the royal palace, many people had already gathered and were waiting to pay the king their respects.

Then, the king walked into the throne hall and took his seat. Everybody, including Soratus, knelt humbly to pay their respects.

“Well, all rise,” said the king.

“Thank you, your Majesty,” the gathering echoed.

Then the king asked, “Soratus, how are you?”

“I am fine, your Majesty,” came the reply.

“Do you know why I asked you to come here today?” the king asked.

“I don’t know, your Majesty,” Soratus answered.

"Because I realize you are getting old. I don't want you to go to war again, I want you to be a hero of Rome. I need your help to train a new batch of commander-in-chiefs to become good leaders to the army like you once were." The king then requested, "Could you advise these young men?"

Soratus replied in a determined voice, "I am more than willing to help our army and nation. It is a great pleasure for me to contribute to my motherland."

"That's great. You have one year to train these young men to be dexterous warriors. Thank you so much, Soratus," The king expressed his gratitude.

"It is my resolution to serve the country and I am honored by your request. I am confident that this mission can be achieved within a year," he promised.

"Excellent! Well then, this meeting is now dismissed," the king concluded.

The gathering was on its knees once again as the king left the throne hall for his personal quarters.

Soratus arrived home and went straight to his working room. He opened his secret chamber located behind the wall and entered the room.

He then picked up a small golden box. It seemed as though it had been untouched for a long period of time as it was covered with dust and spider webs.

The elderly man's wrinkled hands cleaned the box with a small piece of cloth and opened it. There was an old map inside.

"It has been almost five decades since I traveled back and forth along this route. I still vividly remember the events that changed my life," he reminisced.

"Now is an opportune time to hand this map over to the younger generation."

He thought about his glory days with a happy yet enigmatic smile that seemed to hide details that once impressed him.

I would like you to help train the new generation of commander-in-chiefs.

2

THE VALIANT COMMANDER-IN-CHIEF

The next morning, Soratus asked his youngest son, Mosco, to see him in his working room. The father and son preferred to talk in private.

"How old are you, Mosco?" the old man questioned.

"I am 18 years old, father," Mosco answered.

"What do you want to be in the future?"

"I want to serve my country like you did, father," the young man replied with steely determination.

"And why do you want to follow in my footsteps?"

"You are my role model, father. In fact, everybody in this town wants to be just like you. They want to serve their country as soldiers," Mosco's voice was full of passion.

"Do you want to serve Rome?"

"Absolutely, father."

"Then, I have something for you," The old man shuffled through some old papers.

"What is it?" the boy was curious

"It is a map for a great warrior," his father explained.

Mosco was puzzled. "What is a great warrior?"

"A great warrior is one who is able to lead his men forward, boost their morale and protect the nation."

"A great warrior is also a great leader, isn't he?" Mosco asked.

"Exactly!" Soratus replied excitedly. "Becoming a great warrior requires time. One must practice various fighting skills and gather real knowledge, true thoughts, great courage and exceptional goodness."

"Can I become a great warrior?"

"Yes, that is why I called you here."

"How, sir?" the young man asked.

"You have an entire year to travel to this place on the map. Climb to the top of the seven mountains and return home before the year is over."

"Is that it? What will I encounter?" Mosco asked.

"Your encounters will become your experiences. Now is not the right time to know, but when you arrive at your destination, you will understand."

"By the way, father, how did you come by this map?" Mosco asked curiously.

Soratus smiled and said, "I got it when I was young and it made me successful in my work life."

"Is it possible for me to follow in your footsteps?" the boy asked meekly.

"Yes, it is," replied the father with a short laugh. "If you think you can do it, you will be able to. When you trust yourself, you can do anything."

"When should I leave?" Mosco asked.

"You can go tomorrow," Soratus said. "After this trip, you will know good leadership."

Mosco looked up at him thoughtfully and asked, "Have you ever been to this place, father?"

"Yes, I have,' he replied, "at the top of the seven mountains, you will meet those who will tell you how to be a good leader."

"Who are they?" Mosco wondered.

THE POWER OF BELIEF

HELPS US SUCCESSFULLY
OVERCOME DIFFICULTIES.

IF WE BELIEVE

WE CAN DO IT,

WE WILL BE ABLE TO DO IT.

"They are seven angels who will teach you about good leadership, my son."

"Are there really angels in this world?" Mosco was pleasantly surprised.

"You will find the answer to that," the old father smiled. "Now, you should go to your room and prepare for the upcoming journey."

The young man began packing his belongings for the long journey. He would follow the route on the map. He had to solve the riddles behind the seven angels alone, because his father had refused to say anything about them.

Mosco was confident that he would successfully complete his mission. After all, he had to be his father's successor – the new commander-in-chief of the Roman army.

N
W
E
S

3

THE FIRST ANGEL

This was the first time the young man had left his house for a long journey as guided by the map.

The further he traveled from Rome, the more difficult the route became.

He walked past vast fields, sweltering deserts and virgin forests, abundant with wild and fierce animals. Eventually, he reached the first mountain.

THE ANGEL OF DILIGENCE

THE LESSON OF DILIGENCE

As the young soldier climbed the mountain, he stumbled across a large stone slab with a picture of a glass ball and a star in the middle of it. He noted that the same symbol appeared on his map.

As he approached it, a white smoke suddenly rose from behind the large stone. Then, a gorgeous lady in a white dress appeared. She wore a crown and held a long stick.

"Hello, young man. Whom do you wish to see? Can I help you with anything?" the lady asked kindly.

"I am Mosco, and I've followed the path drawn on this map given to me by my father. He told me to gain more knowledge from the seven angels on how to be a good leader," he replied. "How long have you lived here? And who are you?"

"I am Yumin. I live here," the lady said.

"Do you know the Seven Angels? I have come to see them," Mosco confided in her.

She asked why.

"My father, Soratus, gave me a map and asked me to find the seven angels, who would guide me on the path of leadership. I have to be trained to be a great warrior first, so that I can then become a good leader to Rome."

"Soratus?" She seemed surprised. "I know him. We met each other five decades ago and I still remember him very well. How is he?"

"My father is getting old and will retire soon. He was assigned by the king to train the new commander-in-chief. This young man has to be a good, moral and ingenious person, so he can help the king protect the nation," said Mosco.

He then asked, "Did you really meet my father? But you look so young and you are very beautiful," he said, admiring her looks.

The lady smiled, "Yes, I once met your father. When he was a young man, he came here in the quest of knowledge and was destined to meet me."

Suddenly it dawned on the young lad, “So you are one of the angels my father mentioned, aren’t you?”

“People call us that but we simply advise others, as we did your father, Soratus,” she humbly clarified.

“And how do you do that?” Mosco enquired.

I'm Yumin.

"Each of us possesses different disciplines of knowledge. So, we can advise individuals on different issues," she solved the mystery.

Mosco saw his chance and asked, "Is it possible for you to share your advice with me?"

The angel smiled patiently, "Sure, my other name is Angel of Diligence, because I know about human hard work and perseverance. Would you like to learn this trait?" she asked.

"Yes, I would. I have traveled all this way from home to get to know you and gain insight" he said excitedly.

She handed him a book and said, “Take this textbook. Read it tonight and if you have any questions, ask me all of them tomorrow.”

“Thank you so much,” said the young man beaming.

“Alright, I have to go now. I will visit you tomorrow, Mosco,” she said before she was on her way.

Mosco began to look for a place to spend the night. After a while, he sat down wearily, picked up the textbook and began reading under the glistening sky.

He absorbed the essence of each chapter to the fullest from the first page onwards.

LESSON 1

Anyone
can become a leader.

If they are diligent enough,
they can be successful in their work.

People,
no matter their occupation,
can succeed if they start their work
with diligence and patience,
and are not afraid of
difficulties.

Eventually,
they will succeed in life.

THE ANGEL OF DILIGENCE

THE LESSON OF DILIGENCE

LESSON 2

Not all jobs are easy.

But an obstacle
is an ordinary thing.

Those who give in to obstacles
always leave their work incomplete.

These people quit half way.

They won't stand up to fight again.

They will give in and give up
throughout life.

THE ANGEL OF DILIGENCE

THE LESSON OF DILIGENCE

LESSON 3

People must work and constantly acquire knowledge from both small and large details.

They must remind themselves that everything must have a starting point.

Those who think big but fail to achieve their goal, always think that the job at hand is too difficult, too big and unsuitable for them.

THE ANGEL OF DILIGENCE

THE LESSON OF DILIGENCE

LESSON 4

Those who are successful
at what they do
always find ways
and methods to

MANAGE

their work by compartmentalizing
it into smaller parts and then gradually
handling each part
until they have finally and successfully
completed the job.

THE ANGEL OF DILIGENCE

THE LESSON OF DILIGENCE

LESSON 5

People who are lazy at work
end up as failures at the end of their lives.

People who work treacherously
will only get **bitterness** at the end of their lives.

People who sow goodness with their work
will reap **happiness** at the end of their lives.

People who work with
their intellect will harvest
sweet success at the end of their lives.

People who work with all
their heart will harvest
success and **happiness**
during their working life
as well as at the end of their lives.

THE ANGEL OF DILIGENCE

THE LESSON OF DILIGENCE

LESSON 6

People who only use their **mouths**
to work will receive only
unreliable words as a gift from life.

People who rely on **gossip**
to work will only receive the **worst things**
as gifts of thought.

People who use **suffering**
to work will receive the same
as a gift of work.

People who work with **happiness**
will receive an abundance of it
as a gift of work.

People who use **happiness**
to lead their lives will receive
happiness as a gift of life.

THE ANGEL OF DILIGENCE

THE LESSON OF DILIGENCE

LESSON 7

People
who lack **patience**
are no different from **wingless birds.**

Wingless birds cannot fly.

People
with little patience
can accomplish nothing.
They will easily fail
because they are
devoid of strength in their lives.

THE ANGEL OF DILIGENCE

THE LESSON OF DILIGENCE

LESSON 8

Patience is like bricks
that are assembled to build a castle.

The ones with little patience
can only build a small hut.

But others,
especially the successful ones,
have their own castles
that are strong enough to
withstand storms
and cold winds.

These stand majestically,
coping with all kinds of obstacles.

THE ANGEL OF DILIGENCE

THE LESSON OF DILIGENCE

LESSON 9

Patience
leads people to success.

People who want to see
their progeny succeed
need to start training their young ones
about patience
from a tender age.

Patience
is the foundation of discipline.

And people
who lead a disciplined life
always live to treasure
and cherish their actions.

THE ANGEL OF DILIGENCE

THE LESSON OF DILIGENCE

LESSON 10

Leaders
who lack diligence
are the ones with no patience.

When a person loses
due to their laziness,
they tend to blame
everything around them
as its cause.

What they fail to see,
and blame, is themselves
because they have shown no diligence at all.

Happy chirps from countless birds filled the air as a new dawn broke. The sky was illuminated with the first light of the day.

"Good morning, Mosco," the beautiful angel greeted the young man.

He returned her greeting.

The Angel of Diligence then asked, "Did you read the textbook last night?"

"Yes, I did," he replied.

"Do you have anything to ask me?"

"Absolutely," he started. "The first two attributes people need if they want to be successful are diligence and patience, am I right?"

"You are right. All people, no matter what career they are from, can overcome obstacles if they are diligent and persevering," she explained.

"What will happen to those who are not diligent or patient?" he enquired.

She then said, "Diligent men are always diligent. This good habit is instilled in them when they are young. Maybe their parents played a crucial role in teaching them the qualities of diligence and patience."

"Lazy and impatient men refuse to engage in hard work. They merely enjoy an easy and comfortable life. They have been lazy since they were young and when they are older, they can't handle hard work. They are afraid of exhaustion but still want to be rich and powerful. So they end up cheating others to accumulate power and wealth."

Mosco understood the angel. He said, "This means those who enjoy a comfortable life will not be diligent enough to become successful. However, they still want to get a head, so they resort to vicious means to upgrade their social and financial status. They are not good people, are they?"

"That's right. Diligent people are always patient. These traits make them successful. Meanwhile, lazy people also want to be successful but they have no patience. So, they choose only easy and deceitful ways to succeed. Unsurprisingly, bad people can be found in every era," the angel explained.

The young man apparently caught onto something. "You said 'in every era'. Does that mean you've lived here for a very long time?"

"Yes. I was formerly a disciple of Professor Jodum of the Dreams Come True Institute. I pursued my own dreams and have lived for 2000 years. I have seen countless situations, where both good and bad people have lived together. Any community that has a large number of good people will be blessed with happiness. But the one with large numbers of lazy and fraudulent people will be rife with envy, competition and suffering," she concluded solemnly.

"Wow! 2000 years?" Mosco was astonished.

"Yes," she smiled. "Your father asked me the same question once. After I had achieved my mission, another six women also made their dreams come true. Only, we had used different means. I relied heavily on diligence and patience. And so, people began to call me the Angel of Diligence."

"Is there anything else I need to know about diligence?" asked the eager student.

"If you review the contents of the textbook and use its advice as a habit, you are bound to succeed. But that is just the initial stage," the angel assured him.

"Are there many other stages?" Mosco asked.

"Yes, as you travel further, you will meet other angels who can teach you how to live your life happily and successfully," she said.

"I must move along. I need to complete my journey within a single year. Three months have already passed and I've only met the first angel," Mosco said as he stood up to take his leave.

"Yes, you should hurry," the angel agreed, "you still have many leadership lessons to learn and six other angels to meet in order for you to accomplish this."

Mosco thanked the angel with all his heart and said, "I won't forget you. You gave me immense knowledge in such a short period of time. I am very grateful."

"It is my pleasure. I wish you a safe trip and I hope you complete your task on time. Goodbye," she said waving to Mosco as he disappeared in the distance.

Mosco finally said to himself before moving along the path, "Thank you so much. I will make diligence and patience my daily habit."

4

THE SECOND ANGEL

It had taken Mosco three months to meet the first angel. And he was certain that if the map's route would lead him to the second angel soon.

During his journey, the young man tried to read the textbook as often as he could, so that he would remember the lessons and make them a habit. He wanted to remember all of the details when he finally met the next angels.

He stopped at the base of a mountain when he came upon a stone pillar with the same symbol as the that appeared on the map – an image of a crystal ball with two stars inside.

THE ANGEL OF CONFIDENCE

THE LESSON OF CONFIDENCE

Mosco was met by a beautiful woman. She was at the top of the mountain, clad in a long, white dress just like the first angel.

"Hello angel," he greeted her.

"Hello! Are you Mosco?" She enquired.

"Yes, how do you know who I am?"

She smiled softly and said, "Angel Yumin told me about you. We angels always talk with one another. I have been waiting for you. My name is Mindy. I was also a former disciple of Professor Jodum of the Dreams Come True Institute. Now, I am known as the Angel of Confidence."

"I am so glad to have had the chance to meet you," Mosco said gratefully.

"So am I. What can I do for you?"

"I want to be a good leader to the Roman army. I came here to acquire as much knowledge as possible to aid me in my quest of leadership. My father suggested I take this trip."

She understood and said, "I will give you my textbook. After you have read it, you can ask me questions."

Mosco thanked her.

The Angel of Confidence gave him the textbook, realizing that in the five decades since Soratus had visited her, he had never sent anyone on this path.

She pondered that if Soratus had sent his son here, he might have seen potential in him. She also wanted to believe this and help the young man.

Mosco then rested on a large rock nearby and began reading his new textbook right away.

The Angel of Confidence said goodbye and left the young man to read the book alone.

LESSON 11

Confident leaders
can successfully complete great work.

People
who work with no confidence
always fail because
they lack the certainty to do things.

They won't be able to work energetically
because they are afraid of
failures and mistakes.

LESSON 12

Inconfident leaders
will work unwillingly
and always fear they might make a blunder.

They are afraid to make mistakes,
fail, lose and be unsuccessful.

If we keep thinking of bad things,
they might just finally come true.

Not by coincidence,
but because of our own negative thoughts.

THE ANGEL OF CONFIDENCE

THE LESSON OF CONFIDENCE

LESSON 13

Whenever leaders work,
learn or engage in any activity without confidence,
their mission will, in some way or
the other be unsuccessful.

Their unfinished work will
consecutively be done unwillingly
because they are unsure
of the ability to fulfill a mission.

Finally, they will lose
just as they first thought.

THE ANGEL OF CONFIDENCE

THE LESSON OF CONFIDENCE

LESSON 14

Many leaders are confident,
and those who possess this
positive quality are always successful.

These leaders
believe that:

I can do it

I can certainly do it

I must be as successful

I must be as independent as possible

I must be a good person.

THE ANGEL OF CONFIDENCE

THE LESSON OF CONFIDENCE

LESSON 15

People
must have confidence
and should extend
this belief to their team members as well.

People who believe
that sweet success can be reaped by working
and joining forces
will trust all men and have faith
in their colleagues.

Certainly,
they will receive confidence in return.

THE ANGEL OF CONFIDENCE

THE LESSON OF CONFIDENCE

LESSON 16

If leaders lack confidence,
and take actions without it,
the outcome won't be
the same
had the task been done with confidence.

When we believe in ourselves,
we are blessed with bravery.

We will have the courage
to do the right thing
and that is the first step to success.

THE ANGEL OF CONFIDENCE

THE LESSON OF CONFIDENCE

LESSON 17

If we don't trust someone,
don't use his skills.

If we don't believe in his ability,
don't choose him for a task.

If we don't have faith in his abilities,
don't rely on him.

If we are not sure of
his actions, stay away from him.

5

AN OLD BEGGAR

Mosco eagerly continued on his journey to meet the next angel. He had traveled for a long time when he came to a lush forest. Along the path of greenery, he noticed traces of footsteps. This could only mean that people still used this route from time to time.

He went deeper into the forest. Then, he came across an old man seated in the shade. Mosco enquired, “Sir, what are you doing here?”

“I can’t walk any further. My legs hurt,” said the old man. He was dressed in dirty, smelly clothes.

"Where do you want to go?" the young man asked.

"I want to go to the top of this mountain," he replied.

"Oh, then we are going to the same place."

"Ah okay, but you walk ahead. I need to rest."

"Are you going to stay here until nightfall?" the youth asked, concerned for the old man's welfare.

"I can't walk and I don't know what else to do," the old man despaired.

Mosco had an idea. "Let's try this – I will carry you along this path that we both want to take."

“It is better to leave me here. I am but an old beggar and no one cares for me. I haven’t washed myself for over a month. Wouldn’t you find the smell offensive?” the old man asked.

“No, don’t worry, I won’t. See, if I leave you here, you will surely die, because no doctors seem to be passing this way,” said Mosco.

“Thank you so much, young man. I will go with you.”

Although Mosco realized he would have to carry the old man for a long distance, he was willing to do so.

Mosco, with the old man on his back, proceeded deeper into the forest towards the next mountain.

"Young man, what is your name?" the beggar asked.

"My name is Mosco."

"Why are you traveling in this forest?" he enquired.

"My father gave me a map and told me to follow it. He said I could learn how to be a good leader for the Roman Army," answered Mosco.

"I believe you will indeed be a good leader, because you were willing to help even me."

A gentle smile appeared on the old man's lips.

"Thank you. I could not have left you there waiting for your death," Mosco said humbly.

After a while, the old man stopped Mosco and said, "Okay, we are here. This is where I live."

There, the young man saw a large stone pillar that featured a familiar symbol. He was excited when he realized it was like those of the first two stone pillars, "Here it is! This is the place I was looking for!"

"Really? I live here with two of my friends. Would you like to come up? I would be glad to introduce them to you," said the beggar.

Mosco happily agreed.

The young man continued to energetically climb up the mountain, even though the old man on his back seemed to be getting heavier and heavier.

THE ANGEL OF GOODNESS

THE LESSON OF GOODNESS

Eventually, the two men reached their destination. Mosco was exhausted and panting heavily.

The old man thanked Mosco profusely.

Mosco said, "You're welcome. It was no problem at all. We had to go to the same place anyway."

Suddenly, there was a bright white light in front of the old man. Mosco quickly shielded his eyes with his hands. After the light faded, he slowly took his hands away from his face and saw a very beautiful woman had replaced the old beggar.

She asked Mosco, "Is it me you are looking for?"

"Who are you?"

"I am the Angel of Goodness," she replied.

"Were you the old beggar I carried on my back?"

"Yes, you are absolutely right. I simply wanted to test you and you passed, Mosco," she said.

It now made sense to Mosco, "You disguised yourself as a beggar and tricked me into carrying you here."

The Angel of Goodness said, "I didn't mean to deceive you. I merely wanted to test you."

She continued, “People have been looking for me throughout time. But to find me, they had to be willing to help, which they weren’t. Most of them refused to carry me on their backs. Some even ignored me.”

Just then, two more beautiful angels arrived.

"These are the friends I was telling you about," the Angel of Goodness said, "I live with them."

"Hello, young man. You have already passed the test. I am the Angel of Time and this is the Angel of Management. Just take a look at the symbol behind you and you will understand everything."

"I am so lucky to have met all of you," said Mosco.

"You are not lucky. You are a good man. Many people aren't that helpful and don't want to help others like you did," said the Angel of Goodness.

The Angel of Time then elaborated, "That's correct. Most people care only for themselves and are indifferent to lending a helping hand to others. People with no goodness in their hearts will never become good leaders."

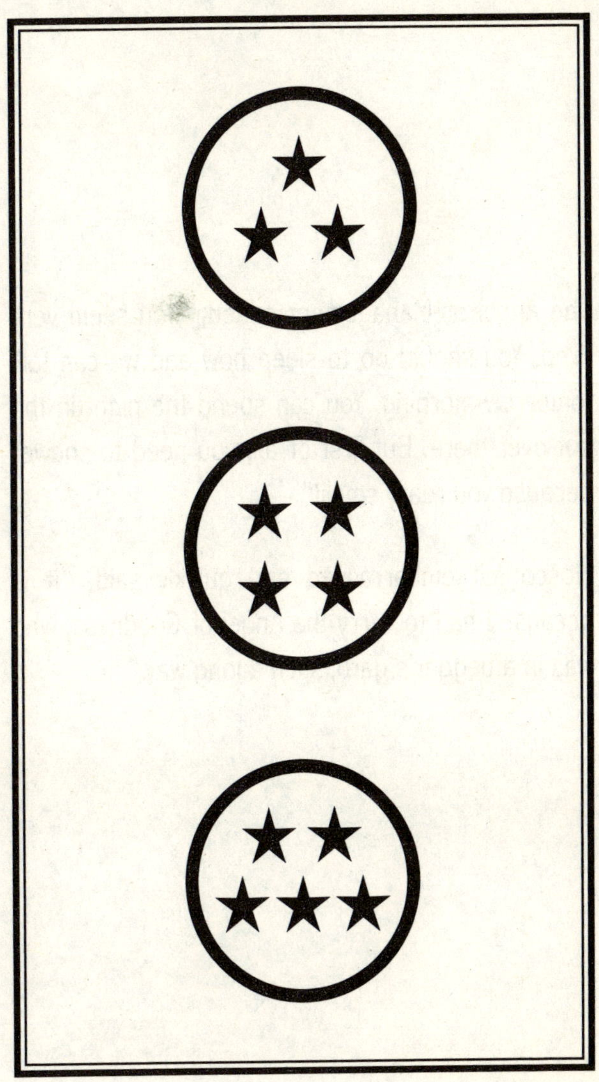

The Angel of Management added, "You seem very tired. You should go to sleep now and we can talk tomorrow morning. You can spend the night in the hut over there. But first of all, you need to shower because you really smell!"

Mosco felt embarrassed and quickly said, "It is because I had to carry the Angel of Goodness, who was in a beggar's garb, such a long way."

“Don’t worry,” the angel replied, “I am only kidding. Sleep well and we can start teaching you everything you need to know tomorrow.”

Mosco thanked them as they took their leave.

“We will meet you here in the morning,” they said.

The three angels disappeared in an instant. The young man walked to the hut and went straight to the shower. He felt ashamed that the angels had mentioned the odor that came from his body.

After the shower, Mosco curled up in bed and fell asleep right away. He was ready to learn the new lessons in the morning.

The Angel of Goodness
The Angel of Management
The Angel of Time

6

THE ANGEL OF GOODNESS

When Mosco woke up, he saw the Angel of Goodness looking down at him.

"Did you well sleep?" she asked.

"Over the past few months, I have rarely had the chance to sleep on a bed lined with soft straw. But last night was very comfortable," Mosco replied.

She was glad and smiled at him.

Then she said, "Here is my textbook. Read it carefully and after you have finished, I will come back to see you in case you have any questions to ask me."

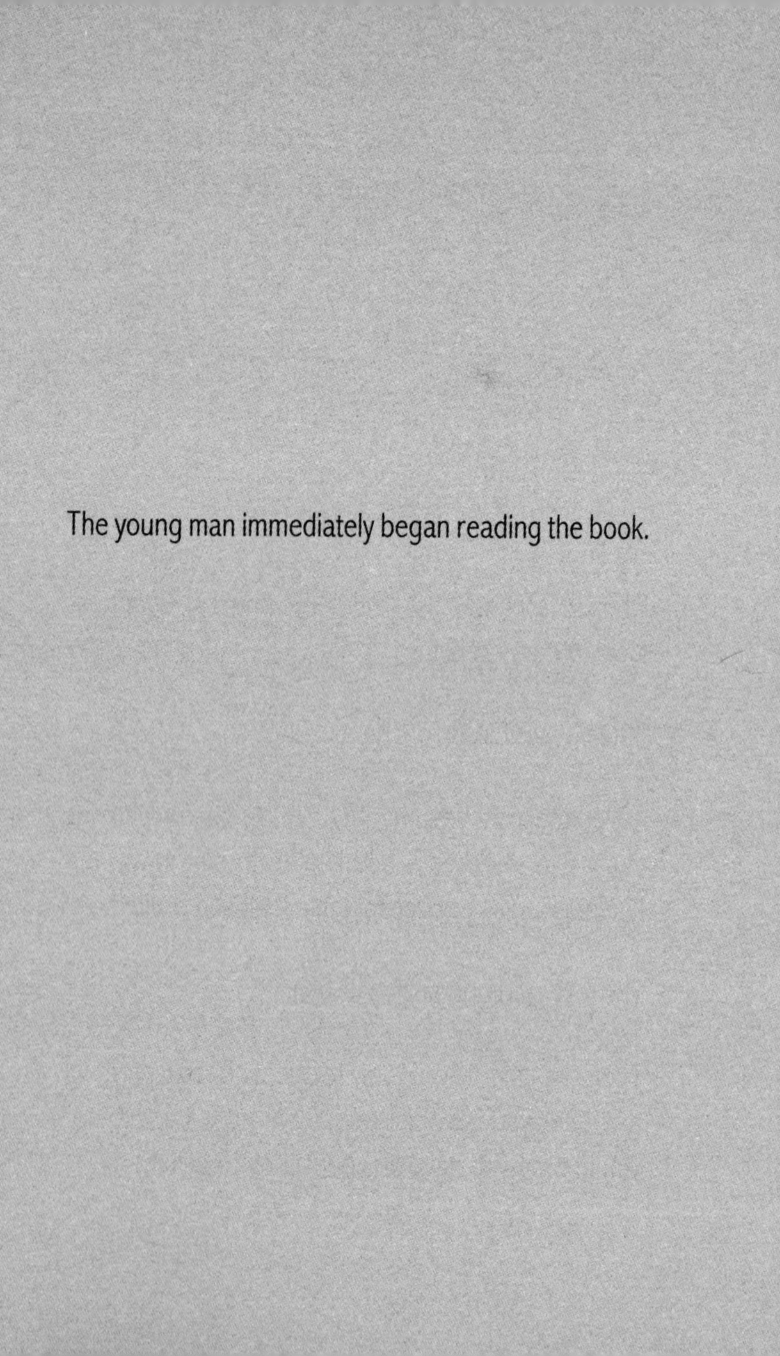

The young man immediately began reading the book.

LESSON 18

Leaders have various things
to accomplish in their lives.

But they always choose to forge ahead,
to the left or the right,
to the north
or down south.

No matter what course
their lives take,
leaders who think and talk good
will receive good things in return.

If bad things are thought and done,
only bad things will happen.

THE ANGEL OF GOODNESS

THE LESSON OF GOODNESS

LESSON 19

People must show gratitude
towards those who have
helped them.

There are countless ways
to move ahead – betrayal or gratitude,
treachery or helpfulness.

Be grateful towards your parents.

Pay gratitude towards your boss

and

someone who gives you a chance
because they believe in you.

Pay gratitude towards your nation.

These are the prerequisite
qualities of all good leaders.

THE ANGEL OF GOODNESS

THE LESSON OF GOODNESS

LESSON 20

A leader who does many good deeds
is like a big tree covered with thick leaves.

Those looking for safe refuge
will always rest under such a big tree.

Birds will build their nests on
the tree's leafy branches.

Ants and insects will forage
for food on a healthy tree.

Every living being can enjoy
the cool and protective canopy of a big tree.

THE ANGEL OF GOODNESS

THE LESSON OF GOODNESS

LESSON 21

Those who have never done any good deeds
are similar to withered trees,
they have no leaves and branches.

When someone needs shelter,
he won't need a withered tree.

Birds
won't build their nests on such a tree.

Ants and insects
won't forage for food here.

No one
would pay any attention to a tree like this.

THE ANGEL OF GOODNESS

THE LESSON OF GOODNESS

LESSON 22

Goodness
comes from the intention
to do something good.

Goodness
can be created with one's own hands.

Goodness
can be fostered
by thinking only good thoughts.

When we think only
about good things,
goodness will happen.

THE ANGEL OF GOODNESS

THE LESSON OF GOODNESS

LESSON 23

Those who do good deeds must
have nurtured goodness since their youth.

Children are innocent
and can be taught
to differentiate between
good and bad.

If a child is not taught how to differentiate
between the two,
they tend to think their actions
are always good,
though what they have done could be bad.

THE ANGEL OF GOODNESS

THE LESSON OF GOODNESS

LESSON 24

Those who make mistakes
might not intend to do so.

They might not have been taught
how to differentiate between
good and bad.

A child
who doesn't know the
difference between right and wrong
or good and bad
could end up seeing white as black.

THE ANGEL OF GOODNESS

THE LESSON OF GOODNESS

LESSON 25

Good deeds
start from a small action.

This is called
the process of fostering a sense of goodness.

When we grow up,
what we have fostered since a tender age
will be in all of our actions.

We later call these actions
morality and ethics.

But before we can possess these two qualities,
we need to start doing good deeds
regularly and consistently.

THE ANGEL OF GOODNESS

THE LESSON OF GOODNESS

LESSON 26

Morality
nourishes society
allowing its people to live happily.

Morality
brings peace and
spiritual happiness to people.

Morality
makes the world a better place.

Morality
can make life more beautiful.

THE ANGEL OF GOODNESS

THE LESSON OF GOODNESS

LESSON 27

A corrupt society
is a place where people live in suffering.

They tend to hurt
and frame one another.

This kind of society
will gradually deteriorate
until it becomes an unlivable place.

Those who live in
such a society, day after day,
will unavoidably feel
gloomy and hopeless.

LESSON 28

Lessons for leaders

Goodness
brings spiritual peace.

Goodness
creates happiness.

Goodness
gives us a refreshed mind.

Goodness
puts a smile on our faces.

Goodness
brings about love.

Goodness
brings liveliness.

LESSON 29

Lessons for leaders

Evil
causes an agitated mind.

Evil
causes suffering.

Evil
causes gloomy feelings.

Evil
causes a melancholic face.

Evil
causes hatred.

Evil
causes depression.

"Good evening, young man," the Angel of Goodness greeted Mosco as he was reading her textbook.

"Good evening, angel. I have just finished reading your book," Mosco replied.

"Do you have any questions? Did any part of the book bring up doubts in your mind."

"Yes, it did. Why do people have to be good? What do good people look like?"

The angel patiently replied, "All people must be good, because there are many underprivileged people in our society. Goodness allows us to sympathize with one another and we learn how to dedicate ourselves to others. People can learn the art of sharing and caring if they are fostered with a sense of goodness."

"If I want to do good deeds, where should I begin?" Mosco then asked.

"We can do good deeds every day by starting with ourselves first. We can think good thoughts both for ourselves and others," said the Angel of Goodness.

"Is it difficult to do good things?" asked Mosco.

The angel nodded, "It all depends on how one is nurtured and taught about having a sense of goodness. Parents need to teach their children how to differentiate between good and bad as both of these will happen to them almost every day."

"But why start with children?"

"Children are much like empty glasses. If we give them good water, they will be filled with good things. But if we give them filthy water, their hearts will be full of dirty and putrid things. And consequently, they will do only evil throughout their lives," explained the Angel of Goodness.

"I understand, but what about adults? Can we teach them good virtue as well?"

"Virtue can be taught to everyone including kids, adults and even the elderly. A person whose head is filled with evil thoughts is just like a glass of dirty water. They can only become better people when they are taught virtuous things, which means pouring in good water. Even then, it will take a long time for the filthy water to be replaced with the clean water necessary to purify their minds. Therefore, it is easier to start with children, who can be molded easily," the angel elaborated extensively to ensure that Mosco understood the concept of virtue.

"Who can teach these things?"

"Virtuous adults can. Good adults can teach children to grow up to be good members of society. An adult who thinks bad will only teach bad things to children. As a result, these kids will not be able to become good people and in turn, they will teach bad things to their young ones," replied the angel.

"How do we differentiate between good and bad people?" Mosco asked.

"It must start with our thoughts first. If we think good, our actions will be good. We should think twice before taking any action to make sure that we don't cause any trouble to others, but benefit the entire society," she explained patiently.

"So, performing good deeds is not difficult, is it? We simply should not cause anyone trouble."

She nodded, "You are right, Mosco. But in today's society, competition is everywhere – at work and in our personal lives. As a result, many problems often arise."

"Are those who do nothing good people?"

"Many people try to avoid getting involved in someone else's problems. A person who does nothing might not be a good person, since people need to take care of themselves and their families by working responsibly to earn money. So those who refuse to do something can cause others to get into trouble by exploiting their assets and money. If we can stand on our own feet and take care of ourselves, we can live happily and be pillars to our family and society," the Angel of Goodness explained.

She continued, "Those who are indifferent to the sufferings of others are somewhat heartless. People have always been selfish. They treasure only material gains, such as money and assets. They don't care about others. And, unfortunately, these kind of people are on the rise."

"Being good should not be difficult, because I always do good things. I have never caused any trouble to my family. I am also diligent," said Mosco.

"That's right," she smiled, "we have to make the people around us happy. We have to offer support when a member of the family is in need. We can perform only good deeds and expand our loving compassion to our neighbors, colleagues, society and then, the entire country."

"I understand it. We have to start with small things first and then expand our noble mission to larger issues. We can then expand our goodness to a wider scope. This can make our society a better place to live," Mosco fully grasped this concept.

"You are right. And when society is livable, our life will be happy," said the Angel of Goodness.

"Thank you so much, angel. Will we ever meet again?" asked Mosco.

"The Angel of Time and the Angel of Management will come to see you tomorrow morning, Mosco. Rest now."

"Thank you. From now on, I will try and only do good deeds and tell this story to all those I know."

"That's good. I believe you can do it. Good luck," the Angel of Goodness said.

"Thank you so much, Angel of Goodness," said Mosco before entering the hut for a night's rest. He would soon see the other two angels in the morning.

7

THE ANGEL OF TIME

AND

THE ANGEL OF MANAGEMENT

Early next morning, Mosco woke up with a refreshed mind. He was eager to learn more new things.

He took a bath and hurriedly dressed. He was anticipating the arrival of the two angels.

"Good morning, young man," said the two angels as they suddenly appeared in front of a startled Mosco.

"Good morning, two angels," Mosco greeted them.

"Are you ready for today's lessons?" the Angel of Time asked Mosco.

"Yes, I am. Previously, I only had the chance to meet one angel at a time. How come both of you have come together today?" he asked curiously.

"We both think that the essence of management and time are important and inseparable. That is why we came together, so we can explain everything to you simultaneously," the Angel of Management replied.

"Here, take these textbooks. Read them both carefully and we will come back in the evening to answer any questions you might have."

"Alright, I will try my best to understand everything, angels," Mosco said.

THE ANGEL OF TIME

THE LESSON OF TIME

LESSON 30

We all get equal time.

But whether or not
time is precious to them
depends on each individual.

Those who are smart
can ensure their time is
spent as wisely as possible.

THE ANGEL OF TIME

THE LESSON OF TIME

LESSON 31

Good leaders will know how to manage their time properly to get the best results.

They will quickly realize whether what they are doing will benefit their lives or not.

THE ANGEL OF TIME

THE LESSON OF TIME

LESSON 32

Time is precious
and it can't be retrieved.

If we are able to
use our time to do only useful things,
we will certainly get useful things in return.

If we spend our time
doing only useless things,
we will certainly
receive useless things in return.

LESSON 33

Countless people don't know
the importance of time.

They simply let it go by uselessly,
wasting it doing trivial things.

As a result,
these people are unsuccessful.

They simply don't know
how to use their time efficiently
for their own sake.

LESSON 34

Good leaders will realize
that they have to study
during their study time.

They have to work
during their work time.

They have to rest
during their rest time.

They have to be happy
at all times!

THE ANGEL OF TIME

THE LESSON OF TIME

LESSON 35

Leaders
who don't see the value of time
often waste it away
paying no attention to it at all.

But at a certain period of their lives,
they will tell everybody
that they regret
the time wasted.

LESSON 36

A diligent leader
can do various things in a day.

A lazy leader
will do nothing but
waste their time indifferently.

Finally,
at the end of their lives,
these two people will get
totally different results,
because they walked different paths.

LESSON 37

Diligent leaders can do
countless things in one year.

And yet, they will always say
they do not have enough time.

On the other hand,
lazy people often say
they don't know what to do
because they are always unoccupied.

Diligent leaders use
their time productively
and produce countless beneficial works.

However,
frivolous leaders will do everything nonsensically.

And before they realize
how valuable their time is, it will be too late.

THE ANGEL OF TIME

THE LESSON OF TIME

LESSON 38

Good leaders,
who behave intelligently,
can bring great benefits to their own lives.

They are able to
efficiently manage
their time.

People
who know how to manage their time
will be able to work efficiently
for the best outcome.

THE ANGEL OF MANAGEMENT

THE LESSON OF MANAGEMENT

LESSON 39

Good leaders
can manage many things in their lives.

When it comes to managing their work lives,
they find good jobs and take care of their duties well.
They eventually succeed.

When it comes to managing their family matters,
they raise happy families and share
their love and happiness
with all the members of the family.

When it comes to managing their assets, they spend
their money wisely and save for a rainy day, too.

When it comes to managing their love, they love life,
they love other people, they love doing good deeds
and they love their homeland.

When it comes to managing their health,
they take good care of their health.
They exercise regularly.
They eat healthy food.

THE ANGEL OF MANAGEMENT

THE LESSON OF MANAGEMENT

LESSON 40

Good leaders
spend their time learning more about how to manage it well.

Acquiring as much knowledge as possible is their duty.

Leaders,
who keep enriching themselves with knowledge, will only accumulate more of it day after day.

Leaders,
who are eager to reap new knowledge, will become versatile and wise people, able to apply their updated knowledge to manage things better.

THE ANGEL OF MANAGEMENT

THE LESSON OF MANAGEMENT

LESSON 41

Leaders
who know how to manage
their time will be
successful in their lives
because they know what to do in
and in what order.

They do the right thing
at the right time
and do not waste
time doing anything unnecessary.

THE ANGEL OF MANAGEMENT

THE LESSON OF MANAGEMENT

LESSON 42

Work
is equally important.

Leaders
who can't prioritize
their work will confuse
their lives.

If they tend to engage
in unimportant work first

and

leave the important work for last,
they will suffer.

LESSON 43

Most people tend to ignore the concept
of management
and think that everything
will automatically become better.

This is not always true.
There are some things that can only be dealt
with if one has the right management acumen.

People need to acquire
more knowledge as it is necessary
to lead an organized life.

But most people always do the opposite.

They tend to know everything,
except the proper management
of their personal lives,
family, health and themselves.

LESSON 44

Good leaders are always
interested in management.

Some leaders always
say that they know everything and are indifferent
to harvesting more knowledge.

Finally, they become
outdated and can't compete
with the new generation, in
terms of management.

Good leaders always admit
what they do not know and try to attain
more knowledge pertaining to it.

THE ANGEL OF MANAGEMENT

THE LESSON OF MANAGEMENT

LESSON 45

Good leaders
know when to move their army forward

and they
know when to move their army back.

Leaders who don't understand
a situation always move
their army ahead when
it should be moved back or stopped,
and vice versa.

THE ANGEL OF MANAGEMENT

THE LESSON OF MANAGEMENT

LESSON 46

Successful leaders
make their plans in advance.

They can predict
how to lead their army.

They know how to strengthen and develop it.

They know what kinds of weapons
are necessary for their soldiers.

To win the battle,
they must get rid of
their army's shortcomings.

THE ANGEL OF MANAGEMENT

THE LESSON OF MANAGEMENT

LESSON 47

Successful leaders
must have enough knowledge
to manage their army and make it powerful.

Unsuccessful leaders
tend to ignore the training of their soldiers
when they are not in combat.

And when a war arises,
untrained soldiers easily end up losing the
battle.

"How are you, Mosco?" the Angel of Management said as she observed Mosco reading her textbook.

"I am well. I have almost finished reading your book," Mosco answered.

"Did you understand everything?" the angel asked.

"Not everything. I have some queries."

"You can ask me anything," the angel offered.

"Why do good leaders constantly need to acquire more knowledge. Is it why they are always the best? Who teaches these brilliant leaders?" asked Mosco.

"In this world, there are many things that we don't understand. Each individual has different abilities. But leaders have to rule the country, its army and its people. They will always try to keep everyone happy and healthy. Some people consider themselves intelligent, so they don't try to acquire more knowledge. These people will never succeed. But people who are diligent and patient enough to learn new things on their own and do so all the time, will definitely succeed. They always keep themselves updated. Their teachers are masters and sages," explained the angel.

"When they become leaders, is it possible for them to listen and believe others?" Mosco wondered.

"That is a very good question. It shows that you are critically thinking and you are sharp." You are right. When someone becomes a leader, he tends to be confident to a certain degree. This confidence will further increase when he succeeds. But if he turns out to be overconfident, then he won't listen to anyone. This is the most dangerous flaw all leaders should be aware of," the angel explained.

"Why wouldn't such leaders listen to anyone?"

"They are blinded by power and, as a result, act this way. When they forget who they are, there is a high chance that they will choose the wrong path and end up misusing their power. Therefore, many leaders succumb to their self-illusion," the angel elaborated.

"So, it is not good to be a leader who forgets himself?" Mosco pondered.

"You are right. Good leaders must not be corrupted by their power, because that can lead to great disasters," insisted the angel.

"Thank you so much, angel. If I ever have the chance to be a leader in the future, I will not forget your advice. I won't be a leader who is completely and blindly dominated by power."

"Very good. Dogmatic leaders lose themselves. When good leaders turn into egotistical ones, they are often misguided by the illusions of power."

"Do all of them fall under the charm of power?" asked Mosco, who was evidently disturbed.

"No, some of them do. Some leaders are consistently good. They are not easily blinded by power."

"I would like to be a consistently good leader. What should I do to achieve this?" the young man asked.

"You have to continually perform only good deeds. The problems of your people should be your prime concern. Good leaders have to be responsible for the happiness and welfare of their people. They must think of the interests of their people first," explained the angel.

"I will remember everything you have taught me, angel," Mosco said full of gratitude.

"You will read and learn further on what I have just taught you in the last chapter. I will leave now. Stay here for the night and then you can continue your search for the remaining two angels in the morning."

"Thank you so much, angel."

"Good luck."

The young man read the last chapter before retiring to the hut to finally rest.

Execute!

THE ANGEL OF MANAGEMENT

THE LESSON OF MANAGEMENT

LESSON 48

Some successful leaders
possess great powers.

Power
is a good thing only when it is in
the hands of good people.

Power
can be harmful
when it is in the hands
of those who misuse it.

Leaders
who are blinded by
their illusory power always end up misusing
it unwittingly.

8

THE ANGEL OF CREATION

AND

THE ANGEL OF LOVE

The next morning, the three angels returned. "Hello, Mosco. Are you ready for your next trip?"

"Hello, angels," Mosco replied. "Yes, I am ready. I have very little time left to find the other two angels. I thank all of you for your kindness and the wisdom you have given me through such valuable lessons."

"It was our pleasure, young man. Good luck," the three angels said goodbye to Mosco.

"Goodbye. Thank you all so much," Mosco bid them farewell and went on his way.

The young man continued on his journey and hoped to reach his next destination soon.

While traveling, Mosco recalled what his father had said to him. His father had been an exceptional commander-in-chief, who once walked this same route and experienced the same things he was now experiencing. After meeting the seven angels, his father had gone on to become the most respected leader of the Roman Army.

His father had experienced good things and was guided by the seven angels' advice on how to be a good leader. So, his father had become a consistently good leader and was loved by his people.

Mosco promised himself that he would try to be a good leader just like his father.

After a while, Mosco noticed a symbol at the base of the last mountain and he was sure that it was where the other two angels lived. He started walking faster.

He was ecstatic to have noticed the familiar symbol on the mountain again.

He expected to meet the last two angels soon.

He would then be able to finally see his father again.

Before that, he wanted to acquire more knowledge. He wondered which angel he would meet next and what she would teach him.

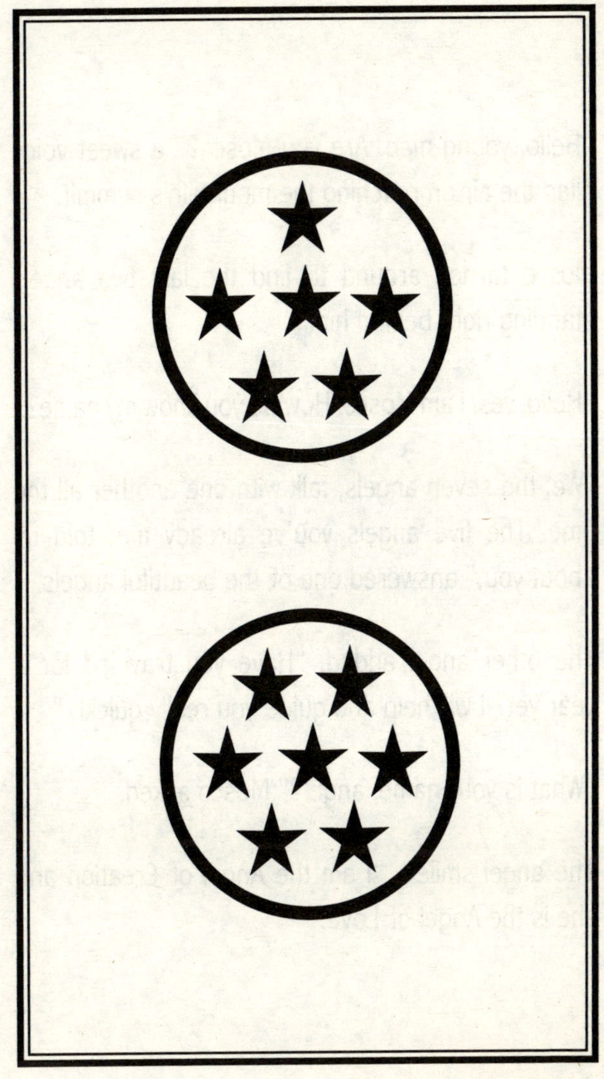

"Hello, young man. Are you Mosco?" a sweet voice filled the air on reaching the mountain's summit.

Mosco turned around to find the last two angels standing right behind him.

"Hello, yes, I am Mosco. How do you know my name?"

"We, the seven angels, talk with one another all the time. The five angels you've already met told us about you," answered one of the beautiful angels.

The other angel added, "Have you traveled for a year yet? I will help and guide you really quickly."

"What is your name, angel?" Mosco asked.

The angel smiled, "I am the Angel of Creation and she is the Angel of Love."

Mosco said happily, "I am so lucky to have met the two of you before my deadline. I can't wait to attain more knowledge from the both of you."

They understood and replied, "We will give you our textbooks now. If you have any questions, you can ask us in the morning."

The two angels handed their textbooks to Mosco and then suddenly vanished.

Mosco picked up the books and started to read them one at a time enthusiastically.

THE ANGEL OF CREATION

THE LESSON OF CREATION

LESSON 49

Human beings
are blessed with a creative mind.

People
who create good things
for the sake of others, create good things
for society as a whole.

Social creation makes
the livelihood of others better.

Social destruction
causes many problems and
worsens society.

THE ANGEL OF CREATION

THE LESSON OF CREATION

LESSON 50

Leaders
who are blessed
with a creative mind
can create new things all the time.

Creative ideas
that are to do with administration
can keep society in peace and order.

Creation in society leads
to social progress.

Any society
that has no creative leaders
will steadily decline.

THE ANGEL OF CREATION

THE LESSON OF CREATION

LESSON 51

A good leader
should have creative ideas
that bring good benefits
to society.

Creative ideas
focused on citizenship
lead to social unity.

Good ideas
bring prosperity to people
and the society
as well as the nation as a whole.

THE ANGEL OF LOVE

THE LESSON OF LOVE

LESSON 52

Love
makes everything
around us more beautiful.

Love
is the source of
inspiration and creation.

Because love
inspires people
to create new things.

Love
makes people
stronger and braver.

THE ANGEL OF LOVE

THE LESSON OF LOVE

LESSON 53

Love is a prerequisite
for leaders.

Love of a leader makes
followers trust them.

Love of a leader
brings confidence to the teams.

Love of a leader
unites the followers
and encourages them to do good things.

THE ANGEL OF LOVE

THE LESSON OF LOVE

LESSON 54

Love in the family
leads to family happiness and unity.

Love in the population
leads to social happiness.

Love among mankind
leads to happiness in life.

Love in work
leads to happiness in the work arena.

Love
brings happiness to everything we do.

THE ANGEL OF LOVE

THE LESSON OF LOVE

LESSON 55

Leaders
who practise and work with
loving compassion can bring
happiness to their work and lives.

They can also bring
spiritual peace and delight to all hearts.

And they can bring
simplicity to life too.

As soon as Mosco had finished reading the last textbook on leadership, all of the seven angels appeared before him.

"Hello, angels," Mosco greeted each one of them.

"We have all agreed that you have gathered enough valuable knowledge. You should use it as a guide to your life, so you can become a good leader, just as you wished to be," the Angel of Goodness said.

"I am very greateful and glad to have had the chance to read these textbooks by each of you. Now I know why my father is a good, capable and confident leader. You gave him the most precious lessons of all," the young man said.

"We are glad to know that your father is a good and successful leader," the Angel of Management replied.

"We hope that you will become a good leader like him," the Angel of Time added.

"I promise that I will try my best to become a good leader like my father," Mosco stressed.

"We hope you achieve your goal, Mosco," the Angel of Love said warmly.

"It is now time for you to return home and do what you have to," said the Angel of Diligence.

"Yes, I will now return home to my father. Goodbye to all of you," Mosco said.

"Good luck, young man," said the angels.

"Thank you so much for guiding me. I wish you all a very happy life," replied Mosco.

All the angels waved goodbye to Mosco.

The young man headed home with the strong determination and confidence of becoming a good and successful leader.

"Thank you so much, Seven Angels."

DAMRONG PINKOON was born in Bangkok, Thailand, in November 1972. He graduated with a bachelor's degree in business administration and a marketing major from the University of Thai Chamber of Commerce, Bangkok, Thailand (UTCC). He also attended the College of Management of Mahidol University (CMMU) from where he graduated with a master's degree in management.

DAMRONG PINKOON started working with Thai Carbon Black Public Company Limited (Birla Group from India) and then moved to Thai Escorp Limited, a Japanese company based in Bangkok, Thailand, with its headquarters in Shinsho Corporation in Tokyo, Japan.

DAMRONG PINKOON started his own business in Bangkok in 1999 called Rester Massage Chair when he was 26 years old. He was a successful businessman and his business became the talk of the town within four years. Today, he has one of the most successful businesses in the luxury seating sector.

After tasting success in business, he began writing many pocketbooks, which became bestsellers in his hometown. As a well-known author, he was invited to speak at seminars, advised other corporations and individuals and became an instructor of business strategies.

His philosophy books and how-to novels have been translated into many languages in the past few years and have since gone on to become bestsellers on the international book scene.

Damrong Pinkoon

Special Thanks

Ms. Sirisara Pinkoon	for all the support
Ms. Daranee Rattanathum	for assisting and corroborating
Ms. Chompoo Trakullersathien	for translation
Mr. Philip Hall	for editing
Ms. Uchenee Puttichard	for assisting

And thanks again for everything
I've learned from all my professors.
And to the great writers who wrote great books,
thank you for making it all possible for me.

JAICO PUBLISHING HOUSE

Elevate Your Life. Transform Your World.

ESTABLISHED IN 1946, Jaico Publishing House is home to world-transforming authors such as Sri Sri Paramahansa Yogananda, Osho, The Dalai Lama, Sri Sri Ravi Shankar, Robin Sharma, Deepak Chopra, Jack Canfield, Eknath Easwaran, Devdutt Pattanaik, Khushwant Singh, John Maxwell, Brian Tracy and Stephen Hawking.

Our late founder Mr. Jaman Shah first established Jaico as a book distribution company. Sensing that independence was around the corner, he aptly named his company Jaico ('Jai' means victory in Hindi). In order to service the significant demand for affordable books in a developing nation, Mr. Shah initiated Jaico's own publications. Jaico was India's first publisher of paperback books in the English language.

While self-help, religion and philosophy, mind/body/spirit, and business titles form the cornerstone of our non-fiction list, we publish an exciting range of travel, current affairs, biography, and popular science books as well. Our renewed focus on popular fiction is evident in our new titles by a host of fresh young talent from India and abroad. Jaico's recently established Translations Division translates selected English content into nine regional languages.

Jaico's Higher Education Division (HED) is recognized for its student-friendly textbooks in Business Management and Engineering which are in use countrywide.

In addition to being a publisher and distributor of its own titles, Jaico is a major national distributor of books of leading international and Indian publishers. With its headquarters in Mumbai, Jaico has branches and sales offices in Ahmedabad, Bangalore, Bhopal, Bhubaneswar, Chennai, Delhi, Hyderabad, Kolkata and Lucknow.

SINCE 1946